**BETTER KARATE**

Tameshiwari: ice-breaking technique demonstrated T. Nakamura (7th Dan) at Crystal Palace, Lond

# Better Karate

Steve Arneil (6th Dan)
Bryan Dowler (3rd Dan)

with 247 illustrations

Kaye & Ward · London
in association with Hicks Smith & Sons
Australia and New Zealand

First published in Great Britain by
Kaye & Ward Ltd, 21 New Street,
London EC2M 4NT
1976

Copyright © Kaye & Ward Ltd 1976

All Rights Reserved. No part of this publication may be reproduced, stored in a retrieval system, or transmitted, in any form or by any means, electronic, mechanical, photocopying, recording or otherwise, without the prior permission of the copyright owner.

ISBN 0 7182 1444 7

Printed in Great Britain by Whitstable Litho,
Straker Brothers Ltd, Whitstable.

# Contents

| | | |
|---|---|---|
| 1 | What is Karate? | 9 |
| 2 | Basic Karate principles you should know | 13 |
| 3 | Karate preparatory exercises | 15 |
| 4 | Karate stances and movement | 18 |
| 5 | Punches and strikes | 31 |
| 6 | Kicks and jumping kicks | 42 |
| 7 | Blocks and defence | 52 |
| 8 | Practising together | 59 |
| 9 | Karate kata | 66 |
| 10 | Equipment training | 73 |
| 11 | The Karate training hall and Karate etiquette | 79 |
| 12 | Choosing a Karate school | 87 |
| | Glossary of Japanese Karate terminology | 93 |
| | List of Karate organizations and associations in Great Britain, Australia, Canada and United States | 95 |

A high roundhouse kick *(jodan mawashi-geri)* performed by a junior Ist Dan of the British Karate Kyokushinkai, 10-year-old Paul Cheeseman.

# Acknowledgements

The authors wish to express their sincere thanks to Brian Bellingham, who took nearly all the photographs for this book at very short notice in spite of the pressure of his business; to Bernard Creton (2nd Dan), to Stephen Jones and Paul Cheeseman (1st Dans), and the other members of the Wimbledon and Croydon Kyokushinkai dojos, who gave great assistance in the preparation of this book.

Master and pupil: one of the authors, Steve Arneil (6th Dan), with a junior student.

Kata — the 'art' in this martial art.

A side jumping kick *(yoko tobi-geri)* performed over a rope.

Instruction in free-sparring *(Jiyu Kumite)* techniques.

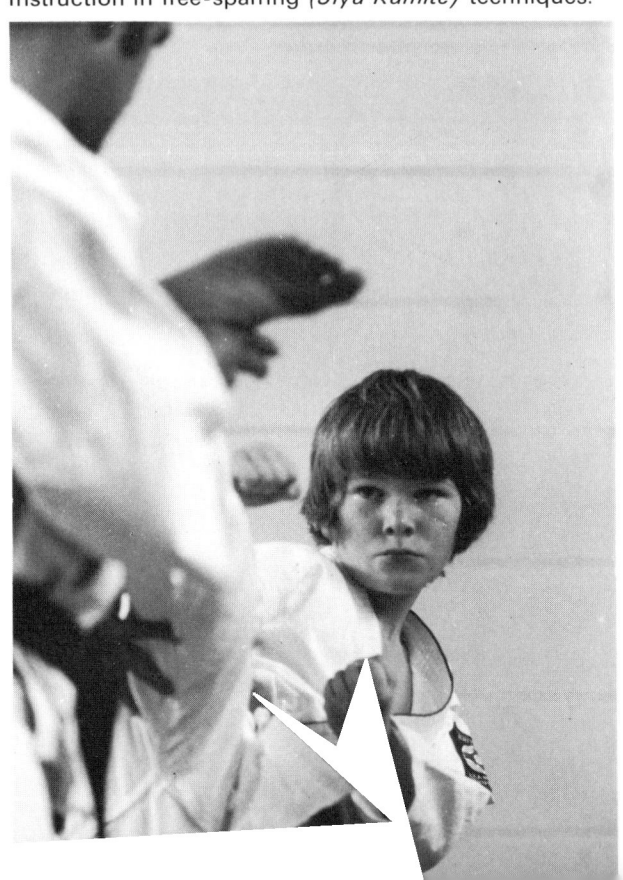

# 1. What is Karate?

Karate is a martial art. To date it is the most effective form of hand-to-hand combat devised by man; it is a form of physical education with mental discipline, a fast-growing internationally competitive sport, and, to a few masters of Karate, it is a concept of a way of life.

The art we now call Karate began in India and China, not Japan — methods of fist-fighting were known and documented in China before the birth of Christ. The methods of combat introduced from India to China by Bodhidharma (known as Darumataishi by the Japanese) in the 5th century AD, and taught by him at the Shaolin Temple, were developed by the Chinese over the centuries into a more sophisticated fighting system. The various Chinese hand-to-hand systems, which varied considerably from school to school (as the various Chinese Boxing styles do even today), were imported to Okinawa in the Ryuku Islands and, after further additions of local techniques by teachers in the Ryukyus, were first introduced to Japan as late as 1917. These particular methods, introduced by the Okinawan masters of unarmed combat, were finally termed 'Karate-do' (literally 'empty-hand ways') and they were categorized by the Japanese into a system of combat training.

Most Asian countries have unarmed combat systems that to some degree have strong similarities with the Japanese and Okinawan systems of Karate; indeed many of the special techniques of these other countries have been incorporated recently into some of the Japanese Karate systems. A specific example of this is the Korean specialised jumping kicks. In China and Taiwan these fighting systems are known as Chinese Boxing and are often grouped together under the term *Kung Fu*. In Indonesia they are called *Pentjak;* in Malaysia *Bersilat;* in Korea *Tae Kwon Do, Tang Soo* or *Hapkido;* Thailand has its own spectacular Thai Boxing with kicking methods which have, in the last 10 years, been incorporated into the professional kick boxing ranks in Japan.

Karate had its earliest roots in Buddhism, and today all serious Karate instruction emphasises the mental discipline expected of students and teachers as well as Karate's physical and martial objectives. This harmonization of the physical objectives and mental discipline makes Karate different from other 'sports' as we usually think of them. It is also different from the hand-to-hand fighting systems evolved in the West, which are usually not linked to any form of spiritual or mental discipline.

Gichin Funakoshi, an Okinawan, who is accepted as having introduced modern Karate to Japan from the Ryukyu Islands, is credited with saying: 'A true student of Karate is one who will practise daily throughout his lifetime and never find the necessity to use his knowledge in anger against another. The ultimate aim of the art of Karate lies not in victory or defeat but in perfection of the character of the participants.'

Karate is, therefore, more than just a sophisticated system of self-defence. Karate can provide you with the opportunity for physical and mental harmony within which is a concept of life which can be the basis of your attitude to other people, to the world and to life in general. The first steps along this road of discovery and self-fulfilment are through the obedience and discipline of the *physical* side of your Karate training. The whole of your early training in Karate is, therefore, limited to the physical aspects of the art.

Many people still think of Karate as a technique for breaking solid objects like wood, stones, bricks and so on. This is certainly done, but it represents only a very limited aspect of Karate activity and philosophy. The breaking techniques are often displayed at tournaments and exhibitions and are called *Tameshiwari.* These techniques are particularly associated with Japanese Karate and the Korean styles. The feats which experts perform publicly show the quite startling penetrative power which can be generated by the body and released through the correct use of the principles of Karate technique. Tameshiwari are not part of Karate proper but serve two main purposes. First, and foremost, exhibitions *test* the ability of the person breaking to carry out the break. This is a practical test of the Karateka's ability to concentrate and to focus his power and technique on a given spot, which is not really possible under standard training conditions against other students as the blows are 'pulled' or 'focused' just short of the actual target. Indeed, in the annual open

A tremendous exhibition of ice-breaking.

tournament in Tokyo of Mas Oyama, the famous Karate master and founder of the Kyokushinkai school, all contestants entering the competition must first complete various practical tests of breaking in front of the audience before being allowed to compete in the tournament at all. Secondly, these demonstrations serve to *show* the dynamic penetrative force which can be generated by the correct use of Karate technique, and are a sober reminder of Karate effectiveness to the sceptic!

Karate is finally, but not least, a martial *art.* This is seen particularly in the requirement that you must learn and perfect the *Katas* or forms. The first few are relatively easy to learn, but the *Katas* become progressively

Group Kata practice.

much harder to learn, perform and perfect. Karate is an art in the same way as *Judo, Jiu-Jitsu, Kyudo* (archery) or *Kendo,* and has the same ethical and moral links as these other martial arts. Like Judo, Jiu-Jitsu and other fighting arts, Karate has, through the progression of human ideas, come to be regarded as the result itself — instead of merely the means to that end, i.e. the swift downfall of your opponent. As a result of this the *Katas,* which are intended to link your basic training with the actual realities of combat, have now assumed their own importance as the artistic side of Karate to such a degree that the postures of the body and the methods of movement have come to be viewed and criticized within the normal standards of aesthetics. So the movements of *Kata* have been progressively revised to show not only the practical side of movement but also the grace and harmony of such movements.

Until very recently Karate was considered a strange Oriental martial system, the principal training for which was thought to be beating parts of your body against blocks of wood and stone until they became hard! Now, in Europe and America, the true philosophies are gradually being understood and appreciated by persons involved in the promotion of Karate as a sport, and by students, as well as by those few masters who have always seen Karate as a way of life. Learning Karate has enhanced life for many westerners in the twenty or so years that it has been taught in America and in the ten years or so since Karate was first demonstrated in Great Britain. We hope that this book will show the 'way' of Karate, will enable you to grasp the basic physical principles and techniques, and at the same time help you to realize the equally important philosophy of the martial arts.

# 2. Basic Karate principles you should know

This book aims first and foremost to give you a basis for tackling the physical side of the art of Karate. You will need to know and understand the main physical principles which underly all Karate technique.

Karate technique has been concisely described as *the practice of concentration of strength at the proper time and place.* There are several points implied in this definition which need to be looked at closely.

## SPEED

Karate techniques must be executed correctly; the techniques must also be carried out with the maximum speed possible. The use of speed will achieve the concentration or *focusing* of the force of the blow.

## CONCENTRATION OF POWER AND FOCUS

The fist, the elbow, the ball of the foot or the heel may actually complete the strike but, in order to generate maximum power, all the strength of the body must be used through its various muscles in sequence.

Some muscles of the body – for example the heavy muscles of the hips and back – are strong but slow in movement. Other muscles of the body – normally the extremity muscles – can be used very quickly but are less strong. The object in your Karate training is to bring the heavy muscles into play first, and transfer this power through your body to the point of impact, which is normally the fist, elbow or foot.

At the moment of impact with the target all your muscles are tensed to focus or concentrate all the body's power at that instant.

## ACTION AND REACTION

An important principle of physics is that every action has an equal and opposite reaction, and this applies to Karate techniques also. The best example of this is in the Karate punch where, as one hand punches, the other is withdrawn simultaneously, adding reaction force to the punching hand.

## BALANCE

To perform well at Karate, as with most sports, you will need to maintain good balance and stability. This is particularly so where kicking is concerned, when you will — for a second or so — be standing on one leg only.

The subject of balance is dealt with in more detail in Chapter 4 dealing with Karate stances and movement.

## BREATHING AND BREATH CONTROL

Breathing is of such obvious importance that it is often overlooked; in Karate training, however, there are special methods of breathing which you will be taught and which you will need to master before you can reach a high grade. The Karate special breathing methods are designed to control body tension and breathing in actual combat situations, and to strengthen the lower abdomen.

In order to concentrate all your strength at the required instant, you will be taught to shout *(Kiai)* at the instant of impact of the strike or block. As you shout, you will simultaneously expel all your breath; this will have the effect of contracting your muscles, thereby maximising the power of your technique.

## TIMING

Good timing can obviously make the difference between a technique falling short of the target area or missing entirely, and therefore being wasted, and the same technique being delivered with focused power on the target.

Good timing is achieved only after long practice and particularly after experience in free fighting and in competitions. Chapter 8 on training together is aimed at helping you achieve correct timing in basic techniques.

# 3. Karate preparatory exercises

The exercises used in Karate training are divided into two basic groups:
- *(a)* Exercises for relaxing and stretching; these are the exercises dealt with in this book.
- *(b)* Exercises for strengthening.

The preparatory, or warming up, exercises of most sports can be adapted for Karate use, but there are special exercises used in Karate training.

The relaxing and stretching exercises for the legs are most important in making the leg muscles supple and soft so that carrying out the kicks will by easy, and maintaining balance during and after the kicks will be made less of a problem. The exercises shown in this book are basic, and numerous others will be incorporated in your training from time to time, in addition to the strengthening exercises which are not shown here. These basic exercises are done at the beginning of your training session to loosen up, and some of the exercises are done again at the end of training to prevent stiffness.

Knee rotation exercise.

Hip limbering exercise.

Hip and leg stretching exercises.

Wrist exercise.

Finger exercise.

Box splits for supple legs.

# 4. Karate stances and movement

To be successful in any sport you must learn good balance. The expert in a particular sport normally maintains such good balance on field or court that the importance of his doing so is not very noticeable. But consider the problem of a soccer or rugby player who, when attempting to accelerate round an opponent, fails to retain his balance when executing such movements.

In Karate the problem is magnified, because your opponent normally is trying to upset your balance in order to gain an advantage. It is, therefore, necessary to become stable in numerous positions, as you will not always have time to shift into the stance or position you would choose when facing an opponent. Ultimately you must be able to defend yourself from several attackers approaching from different directions. The ability to turn rapidly yet maintain good balance and composure in a multiple-attack situation is one of the pinnacles of ability that Karate students seek to reach.

### READY STANCE (Fudo Dachi)

As with all stances, the body is pulled tight, particularly the waist, hips and legs. There are no stances in Karate where the body is limp.

*(far left)* Note the feet position.

*(left)* Note the position of the head and the height of the hands.

In addition to achieving good balance, the purpose of most stances is to assist in building powerful legs and hips. Strong legs and hips are of great importance to the Karate student, because of the premium placed on leg techniques and the use of the hips in Karate. The most important stances only are detailed in this book.

## FORWARD LEANING STANCE (Zenkutsu Dachi)

A very stable stance if done correctly; it is consequently taught at an early stage. The feet are shoulder wide, and the rear foot is approximately two shoulders back.

A front downward block with the forward arm is usually completed simultaneously as you move back into this stance.

## BACK LEANING STANCE (Kokutsu Dachi)

It is important to understand the way in which your weight is distributed in this stance: about 70% of your weight will be on your rear leg, and about 30% on your front leg.

The back leg is well bent, the foot placed at an angle of 45° to the front; the forward leg is about three feet in front of the rear leg and very slightly to the side. The front knee is raised until the front heel lifts off the floor.

## CAT STANCE (Neko Ashi Dachi)

This is similar to the Back Leaning Stance, but the front leg is brought closer to the rear leg, and the front foot is raised until it is in an almost vertical position. The rear leg will be bent back as in the Back Leaning Stance, but nearer to 90% of your weight will rest on the back leg.

## STRADDLE STANCE (Kiba Dachi)

A good stance for building basic power in the hips and legs. The legs are between $1\frac{1}{2}$ and 2 shoulders' width apart. The feet face forward parallel and 'pull' towards each other; the knees push outwards as far over the feet as possible. The hips are pulled forward and the trunk of the body is vertical.

## HOUR-GLASS OR SANCHIN STANCE

In this stance the body, arms and legs are tensed (torqued) very tightly. The knees are

well bent along the line of the feet, which are turned in at an angle of 45°. The stance is used for building all-round strength.

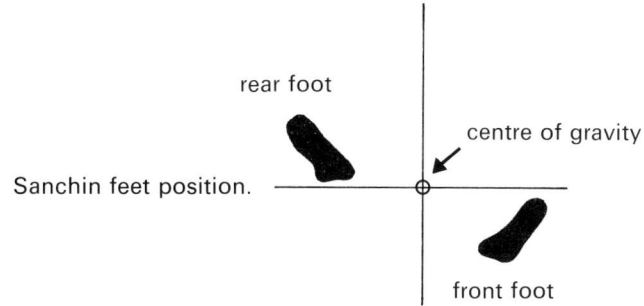

Sanchin feet position.

## MOVEMENT

In Karate training much emphasis is placed on *correct* movement, i.e. changing your stance or position whilst retaining good balance and stability. Without balance and a stable position you will not be able to block, punch, kick or carry out any technique or combination of techniques *effectively*.

In movement there are two main points to keep in mind. First, the feet slide from their position — they are not lifted from the floor (except to execute a kick). To make your movements in bare feet easy, most Karate training halls have polished and sprung woodblock floors. Secondly, the hips and head remain at approximately the same height all the time, i.e. they move forward or backward in a level position. The body does not bounce up and down as it shifts from one position to another.

## TURNING

The greatest test of your ability to maintain balance is in turning your body to face in a different direction — particularly if at the same time you are being harrassed or attacked by an opponent. The important principle is to turn with your *hips;* do not throw your shoulders round or you will overbalance.

The examples of movement and turning shown in this book are in the Forward Leaning and Back Leaning Stances.

Assume the forward leaning stance, turn the heel of the front foot inwards, leaving your weight on the ball of that foot.

The rear leg advances, maintaining the shoulder-width position of the foot.

The rear leg slides through to complete the movement and become the front leg.

## MOVEMENT IN FORWARD LEANING STANCE

**Points to note:** The head or hips move forward (or backwards) in this and all stances at the same height; in other words your body does not bob up and down. The hips are thrust strongly forward with each step and 'lock' into a strong position at completion of the movement, aided by the 'new' rear leg straightening (see photograph opposite).

In the photographs above, you can clearly see the 'square' starting and finishing position of the movement, and also that the feet do not move in and out as you advance or retreat, but maintain the same shoulder-wide position throughout.

Similar movement forward with the other leg.

A reverse punch (gyaku-zuki) executed in a forward leaning stance.

FROM SIDE

**TURNING IN FORWARD LEANING STANCE**

FROM FRONT

1      2

1  Maintaining the same head and hip levels, and with the trunk still facing forward, move your foot across to a position one shoulder's width (approx) from the line of the forward foot's heel.

The important factor is to ensure that your legs and hips execute the turn, your shoulders turning as a result of the hips rotating, and not vice versa.

3

4

2/3   Using your *hips* to rotate, turn the trunk and legs in a half circle, making sure you turn your head first.
4     Snap your hips tight into a 'square' position, your front knee being bent into the correct position, and the back leg straight with the heel pressed firmly to the floor.

Assume the back leaning stance.

Place the heel of your front foot on the floor at an angle of 45° to the front.

Transfer your weight to the front leg and slide your back leg through.

## MOVEMENT IN BACK LEANING STANCE

In all stances it is necessary to maintain the correct distances between the feet both forwards and sideways.

In the Back Leaning Stance, the distance forwards between the feet is about two feet measured from the toes of the rear foot. If this distance is shortened, the stance becomes less stable. The distance between the feet looking from the front is about $1\frac{1}{2}$" to 2" only. If this narrow measurement is reduced, the stance becomes very weak laterally because the feet are directly behind each other as though you were standing on a tightrope.

The same principle applies to the Forward Leaning Stance. In the two photographs opposite you will see that in one a very slight push with one finger is sufficient to upset the student's balance, while in the other the stance is correct and a quite strong push with both hands is insufficient to upset the student's balance.

Keeping the correct weight distribution, place the ball of the front foot on the floor and lift the heel.

Repeat the movement with the other leg.

Here the feet are in a direct line with resulting lack of balance.

The feet are correctly positioned so that the stance is stronger.

Retain the normal weight distribution (70% back leg, 30% front leg) and shift your front foot to a position to the side of the rear foot but in the same line as the original position.

Commence the turn by rotating your hips.

Shift your weight predominantly on to the front foot, placing the heel on the ground.

The back foot is moved in a straight line across and past the line of the front foot.

Turn your body 180° by rotating your hips.

There are two methods of turning in this stance: by moving the front leg or by moving the back leg. The photographs across the top show the first method, moving the front leg; the second method is shown in the bottom row of photographs.

Continue until 180° turn is completed; at the same time shift 70% of your weight to the rear leg. Sink slightly lower by bending the back leg at the knee to counteract the natural tendency to straighten the legs on the turn.

Complete the turn and ensure you maintain good balance.

**TURNING IN BACK LEANING STANCE**

Remember that the important consideration in all turning movements is to utilise the *hips;* the shoulders must follow the hips and not lead them.

Dodging under a high kick and executing a reverse punch (gyaku-zuki).

# 5. Punches and strikes

Most parts of the body can be used as a weapon if circumstances require it, even such unlikely areas as the hips, the shoulders, the shin of the leg and the back of the head. In this book we are seeking to cover the main striking surfaces — the foreknuckles of the fist *(seiken);* the back knuckles of the fist *(uraken),* which are sometimes called the inverted fist; the edge of the hand *(shuto);* and the elbow *(hiji).*

Throughout your Karate training you will be expected progressively to make a tighter and tighter fist. A badly formed or loose fist will be damaged if striking any hard object — and can sometimes be injured even striking the sandbags. A correctly formed fist is therefore essential.

**FORMING A FIST**

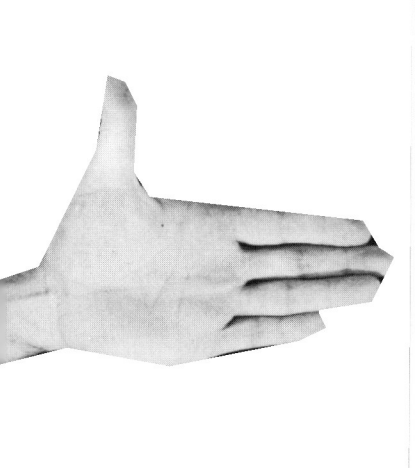 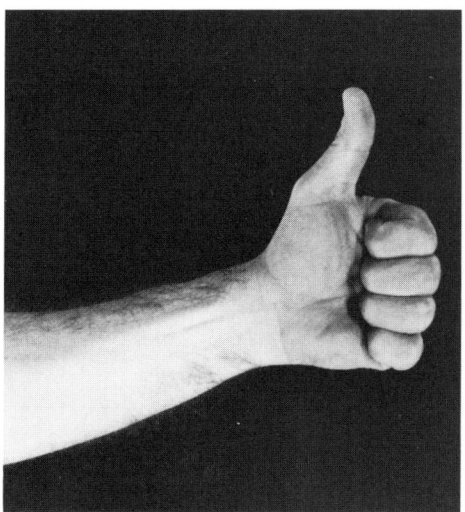 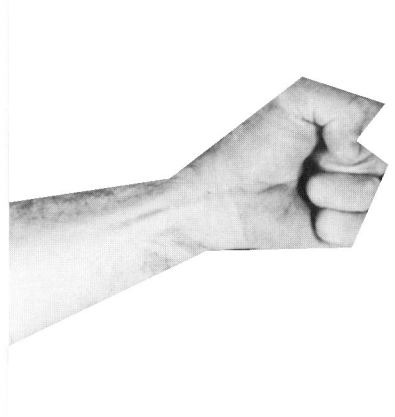

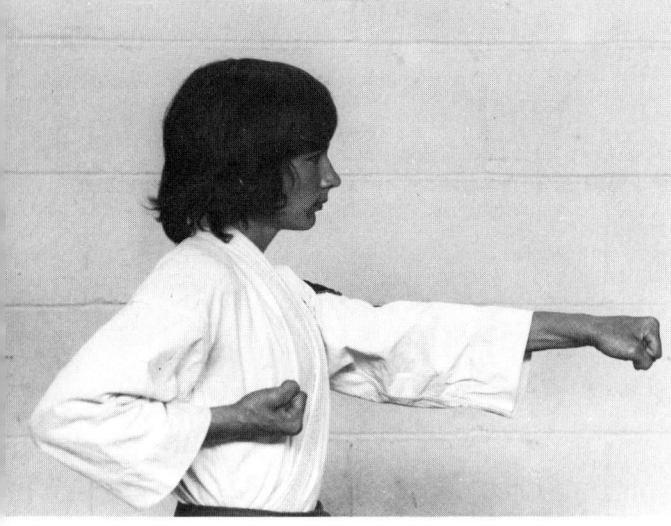

Middle thrust punch.

Lower thrust punch.

The shoulders should not be thrown forward or lifted. The Karate punch uses the hips, back muscles and latissimus dorsi muscles principally, which should be tensed at the moment of impact.

Upper thrust punch.

Reverse thrust with forefist. Note how the shoulder has been kept low.

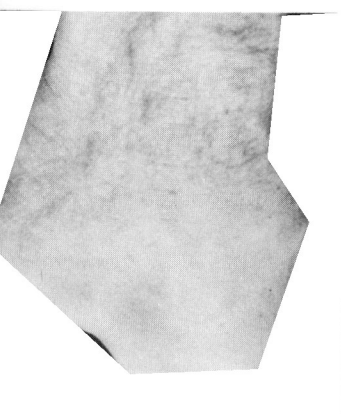
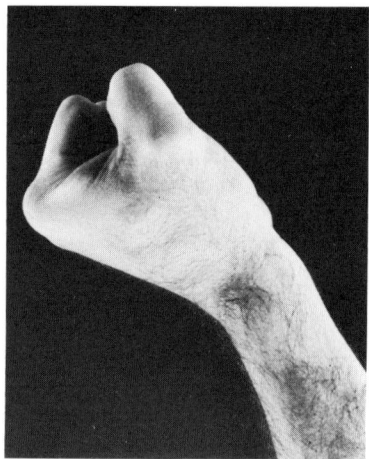

Forefist.    Inverted or back fist.

## Forefist Strike

As one arm punches, the other arm is simultaneously retracted. The punch is executed with a twisting motion of the fists and wrists immediately prior to the instant of impact to achieve maximum penetration.

Commencing position for forward strike.

The same strike shown from the side.

## Back or Inverted Fist Strike

The Back Fist Strike can be made to your front — as in the photographs above right — or to the side; in either case the striking arm is snapped back to the commencing position immediately the strike is completed.

The strike: the arm should not be completely extended. Return arm to first position quickly.

The strike: the arm must not be completely extended. Return arm to the first position quickly.

## Roundhouse Back Fist Strike

As you will see from its name, this a a 'roundhouse' or circular strike with the fist, the striking fist describing a circle from behind the body to the target (normally the head). Power is added by the other arm simultaneously snapping back to the ready punch position and a turning twisting movement from the hips as the fist is about to connect.

Commencing position.

Attacking arm moves behind the lower back; the other arm covers the body.

Both arms move in a circle.

Completion of the strike.

Commencing position for strike against head.

One arm covers the body while the other is taken behind the head.

The striking arm describes a circle.

The strike against the opponent's head.

### Edge of Hand (Knife-Hand) Strike

The striking area is the bone at the base of the edge of the little finger, or the 'meaty' area just above it towards the little finger. The areas to strike against are the opponent's head (just above the ears), the collarbone (as below) and the spleen. The fingers of the striking hand should be kept tightly together and the little finger should not be allowed to pull away on impact.

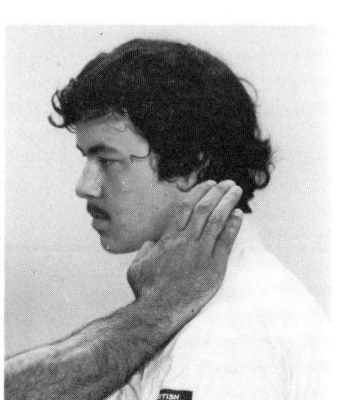

40

Your opponent holds you around the arms.

Use a strike to the rear with your elbow to release grip.

### Elbow Strike

The elbow is a very powerful weapon, particularly useful where the attacker has closed in on you to prevent the use of your kicks.

Every time the basic punch is practised the student is also performing an elbow strike. As the punching arm advances so the other arm is retracted to the ready punch position with a snapping, twisting motion, which creates an elbow strike to the rear (see pictures above). The elbow is normally used to your opponents head and upper body.

To the body.    To the head.    To the back.

# 6. Kicks and jumping kicks

Since kicks must be performed with one leg raised, the importance of maintaining good balance is vital. The supporting leg must be firmly on the ground, and the ankle, knee and hips must be strong and taut to maintain the body in balance. There are some general kicking rules which you must bear in mind:

1. At the start of the kick, the knee of the kicking leg must be raised — the higher the height of the target the higher the knee should be raised. The leg in this movement should be kept close to the body.
2. The knee of the supporting leg should be bent during the kick.
3. The hips should be kept low and thrust in the direction of the kick for maximum power.
4. The kicking leg should be withdrawn immediately after execution of the kick to assist in stability and to guard against your opponent recovering and grabbing your foot or leg.

## FRONT KICK WITH THE BALL OF THE FOOT

Lift knee high, control hands.

Extend leg.

Toes back, but foot extended forward.

Return leg to first position and then to floor.

The Front Kick shown on the previous page is to the opponent's mid-section. The kick shown in the first photograph on the opposite page is a Front Kick at a 45% angle up from the horizontal. Note how the hands aid balance.

## HIGH KICK WITH THE BALL OF THE FOOT

In this kick, which is primarily for strengthening the legs, hips and lower back, the leg swings like a pendulum; the foot is again pointed and the toes are back.

Starting position.

Note that the leg is not bent at the knee.

Kick as high as possible.

A high roundhouse kick shown from the front.

Raise the knee high and stamp down with the side of your foot.

## KICK WITH SIDE FOOT TO THE KNEE

This is used both for strengthening the hips, and as a very powerful close-quarter weapon. In this kick (and in the kick to the waist shown below) the edge of the foot is used; the big toe is raised, but the other toes and the rest of the foot are turned downwards.

## SIDE KICK TO THE WAIST OR ABOVE

A high side kick countered by a side kick towards the waist.

Seen from the side.

Seen from the front.

# ROUNDHOUSE KICK

This is a more difficult kick for beginners to master as it requires very good balance, necessitating co-ordination between the lower and upper parts of the body when the hip is rotated during the kick. Do not allow the upper part of the body to lean back — tensing your abdomen muscles will help to keep the body upright.

Lift your knee high to the side.

Rotating the hips, swing the leg in a circle forward.

Strike with the ball of the foot.

A high roundhouse kick; note the position of the back foot.

## BACK KICK

To master this kick you will need good balance.

It is not always easy to be accurate with this kick and it is, therefore, essential to see that the hips are correctly positioned and aligned (see photograph below). As with all Karate kicking techniques, the hips are used to add thrust.

First, lift your knee to the front and at the same time turn your head to look to the rear. Second, thrust back with the leg and hip, and strike with the heel. Try to avoid leaning too far back when executing the kick. Finally, look to see whether the kick has been accurate and, as always, snap the leg back to the starting position immediately the kick is completed.

The strength of the back kick is that it is difficult to block. The defender should try to shift his body to the side of the attacking leg rather than use his hands and arms to block.

## JUMPING KICKS

Such kicks are spectacular to see and may take an opponent unawares, but they can place the attacker in a vulnerable position unless they are properly executed.

Generally the object is to leap high, kick at the peak of the leap and land *on balance,* ready to continue. It is essential to maintain your balance in the air and on landing, therefore the body should lean in the direction of the kick, rather than away from it.

Jumping kicks can be any of the main kicks: forward, side, round and back kicks.

A side jumping kick is performed over an out-distanced side kick. Note how the jumper's lower leg is being used to cover the groin.

# 7. Blocks and defence

The principal objective of the block is to *deflect* the attack and at the same time leave the defender not only safe from the attack but also in a well-balanced position, allowing him to retaliate, if necessary, before the attacker begins a further attack. If a block is performed strongly with correct timing, it may have such a stunning effect on the attacker that any further step in retaliation is unnecessary.

## UPPER OR RISING BLOCK

Cover the centre of the upper body with the arm.

Place the other fist in front of the covering arm.

Raise the blocking arm.

Thrust upwards firmly using the legs and hips to add power.

The completed block against an attack to the head. Note the blocking arm is in front of the head, not level with it.

## MIDDLE BLOCK FROM OUTSIDE

Cover the upper body with one hand. Take the blocking arm behind the head.

Swing the blocking arm across the body . . .

## MIDDLE BLOCK FROM INSIDE

Commencing position.

twisting the arm and wrist inwards.

Complete the block right across the body.

The completed block against an attack.

Pull blocking arm across the body, twisting the thumb edge of the fist to the outside.

The completed block against an attack.

Starting position; note one hand is already covering the lower body.

Block across the body; the other arm returns to the ready punch position.

## LOWER BLOCK OR PARRY

This is normally used to deflect kicks to the waist and lower body. All the blocks shown can be used against punch or kick attacks. Against some kicks, however, it may be necessary to use both hands, because of the strength of the kick. (See photographs above, opposite and overleaf).

The completed block.

Cross hands block against a kick; note how the defender's body is held firm.

Crossed hands block against a downward blow.  An open hand block up.

A block down with the palm of the hand.  Blocking with the shin.

# 8. Practising together

One advantage you will find that Karate has over many sports is that you can do much of the training by yourself. Punches, kicks, Karate forms *(Kata)* or the use of the punching bags can all be practised without any partners once you have received instructions from your club instructor. You can train in a spare room at home, in the garden or in a local park. If you live near the Karate school you may even be able to obtain the instructor's permission to train in the school if it is not being used on certain evenings or at weekends.

There are times, however, when a partner is necessary. To gain experience in timing your defensive moves, anticipating an opponent's reactions and for simply practising blocking an opponent's arm and leg attacks, a partner is obviously essential. In this book we have divided the suggested *basic* training-together methods into three groups:

- *(a)* Training with both partners stationary.
- *(b)* Training with one partner making a single attack, the other blocking. As proficiency is achieved in blocking the attack, the defender will retaliate against the attacker immediately following the block. This is called 'one-step' sparring.
- *(c)* The third group is similar to (b) except that there will be three steps forward by the attacker — each step being accompanied by the same attack, and three steps back with a block on each retreating move by the defender. After the third block, the defender will retaliate with a strike against the attacker. This group is called 'three-step' sparring.

Each partner will perform in turn as attacker and defender to gain experience.

Start the movements in each group slowly but firmly. Remember that it is each partner's function to help and co-operate with the other. To slip a punch or kick through on the sly, or to strike your partner when he has been distracted does not win any prizes or friends, nor is it within the spirit of Karate. As you and your partner gain experience in the timing of the various attacks and blocks, and pass through the grading system towards black belt, the techniques will be carried through with more speed, power and effectiveness, and at this later stage it is up to your partner to block or dodge the attack without excuses!

## (a) BASIC TRAINING WITH BOTH PARTNERS STATIONARY

This is the starting position facing each other. You should be close enough to be able to strike your partner in this position unless he or she blocks your attacking move.

**1.**

*Attacker*
Left-hand punch to face.

*Defender*
Upper block with right hand.

**2.**

*Attacker*
Right-hand punch to face.

*Defender*
Upper block with left hand.

**3.**

*Attacker*
Left-hand punch to solar plexus.

*Defender*
Right hand performs middle outside block.

**4.**

*Attacker*
Right-hand punch to solar plexus.

*Defender*
Left hand forms middle outside block.

**5.**

*Attacker*
Left-hand punch towards groin.

*Defender*
Right hand makes downward block.

**6.**

*Attacker*
Right hand makes similar punch.

*Defender*
Left hand makes downward block.

At the end of the practice both partners return to the ready position and change roles: the attacker becoming the defender and the former defender attacking.

You should exercise caution when you first begin to practise these basic sparring movements, but ensure that a full technique is carried out. If attacking, do not punch to miss your partner, but rather punch at him or her at a speed which allows your partner time to block and build confidence in his or her ability to deflect or parry the attack. As your partner's confidence increases with his ability to block you, then increase the speed and power of the attack.

## (b) 'ONE-STEP' SPARRING

In all the examples given the attacker will commence from the forward leaning stance *(zenkutsu dachi)*. The defender will move back in the same stance.

Attacker steps forward with upper punch; defender steps back and blocks with an upper block.

Defender immediately returns the attack with an upper punch.

Attacker steps forward and attacks with middle punch; defender moves back and blocks with middle outside block.

Defender retaliates with elbow strike to attacker's body or jaw.

Attacker steps forward and punches at defender's head; defender blocks with an upper block, taking other arm behind his head, and . . .

. . . strikes to attacker's head with edge of hand blow.

Attacker does middle kick at defender's waist; defender blocks with downward parry, at the same time keeping his other hand in the ready punch position.

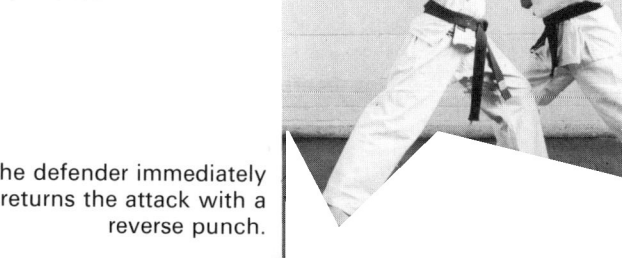

The defender immediately returns the attack with a reverse punch.

# 'THREE-STEP' SPARRING

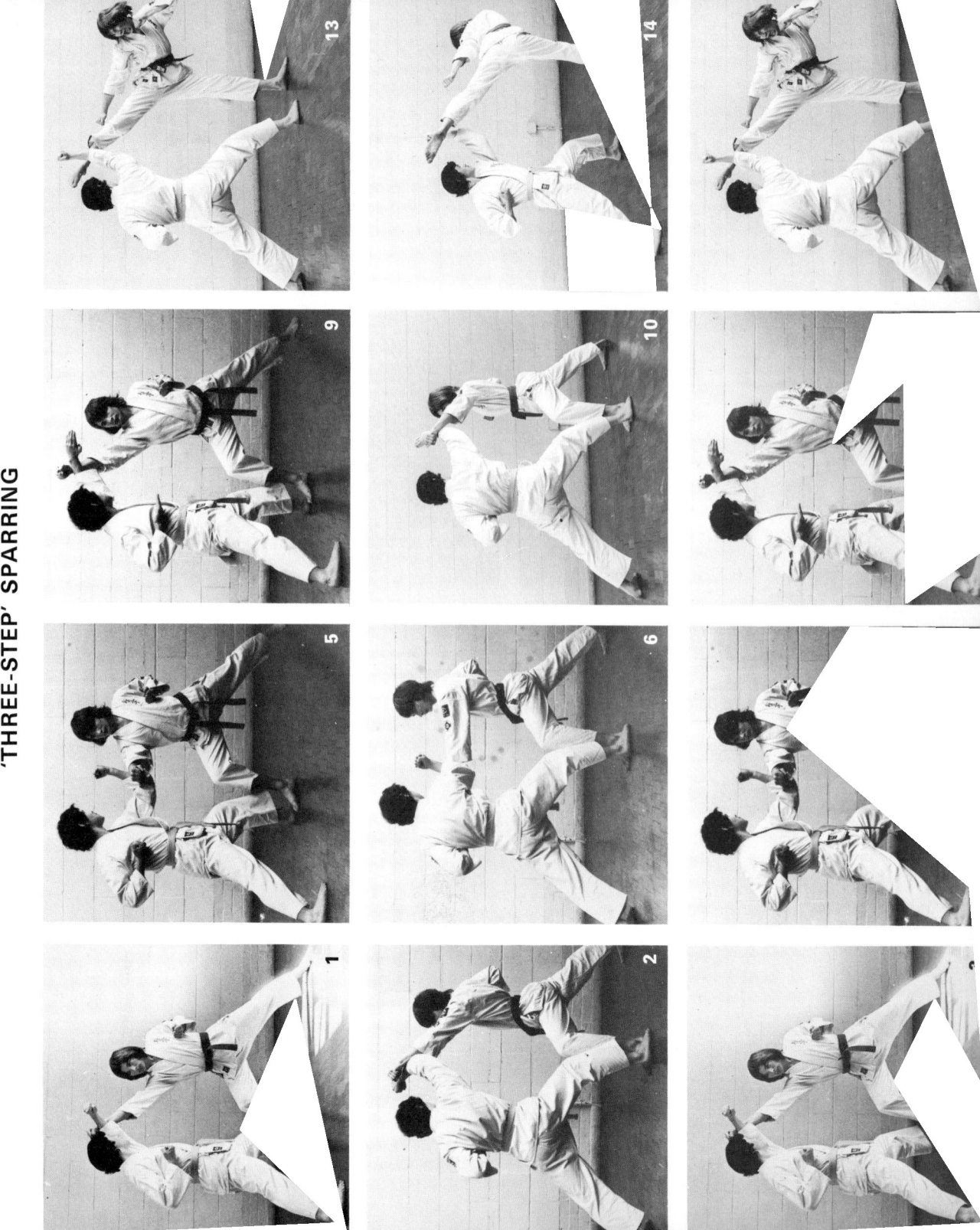

1–4. On each move the attacker leads with an upper punch; the defender blocks with an upper block. After the 3rd attack and block, the defender retaliates with a right leg roundhouse kick to the head.

5–8. On each move the attacker strikes with a middle punch; this is blocked with a middle outside block. After the 3rd attack and block, the defender steps slightly to the left of the attacker and retaliates with a reverse punch to the attacker's ribs.

9–12. An upper punch attack on each step is parried with an open hand upper block. After the 3rd block, the defender pulls the attacking arm forward and downward to unbalance the attacker and retaliates with an elbow strike to the jaw.

13–17. The attacker uses a high round-house kick. This is blocked with the defender's arm across the body. Note that the defender has reversed his leg position. After the 3rd kick and block, the defender effects a back knuckle strike to the attacker's face and . . . then follows up with a reverse punch to the solar plexus.

The examples shown above are intended to give an indication of the numerous movements, attacks and counter-attacks which can be practised in 'one-step' and 'three-step' sparring.

The main objective is for you to become fluent in movement. The pre-determined methods of sparring will help you to link blocking and offensive techniques, and generally shorten your reaction time.

It is important that the style of both the attacker and the defender should be good. The stances should be strong and deep; the hips should be behind the blocking and attacking movements. All techniques must be fully completed even though the strikes are 'focused' just short of the target.

# 9. Karate kata

In the Kata a number of pre-determined attacking and defensive movements and techniques are performed in a fixed order, to a pre-arranged time limit. The intention is to show the most perfect style and form possible, with every movement and technique performed exactly as laid down by the head instructor of the style, or school, of Karate which performs this particular Kata.

Some of the Kata are basically the same as they were when they were devised many years ago. Only peripheral changes and minor revisions have been made to the Kata by the senior masters of a style over many years. One of the most famous Kata practised by Okinawan and Japanese Karate students is *Kanku* or *Kusanku.* Kusanku was the name of a famous Chinese instructor who came from China to Okinawa and taught some of the most notable Okinawan Karate masters.

Kata will assist you as a beginner to learn the basic techniques while moving, thereby affording you a bridge between basic techniques done in a static standing position and 'one-step' and 'three-step' sparring, and ultimately free-fighting. The Kata represent the 'Art' in Karate and indeed, when performed by a master, these Karate 'dances' will thrill audiences of both experienced Karate practitioners and people who have no knowledge at all of this martial art. Notwithstanding the fact that the Kata can be regarded as dances, the speed and force with which the techniques are executed will leave no doubt in the observers' minds as to their effectiveness if they were to be used in combat.

Some styles of Karate have as many as fifty Kata; some as few as fifteen. Some Kata have different purposes. They may be for building speed in movement; others may contain little leg movement but are based on old dynamic tension exercises and are practised to develop basic strength in the student's body.

The three Kata first taught to beginners are the Taikyokus I, II and III. These are simple body-control exercises in an easy-to-follow movement pattern using simple blocks and straight punches. The Kata shown in this book is Taikyoku III, which uses: two stances, the Forward Leaning *(zenkutsu dachi)* and Back Leaning *(kokutsu dachi)* Stances; two punches the Middle and Upper *(chudan tsuki* and *jodan tsuki)* Punches; and two blocks, the Downward Block *(mae gedan barae)* and the Middle Inside Block *(chudan uchi uke)*. The pattern of Taikyoku III, i.e. the foot movements, is similar to the figure I and the time allotted for completion of the whole Kata is 28-30 seconds for a beginner.

**FOOT MOVEMENTS**

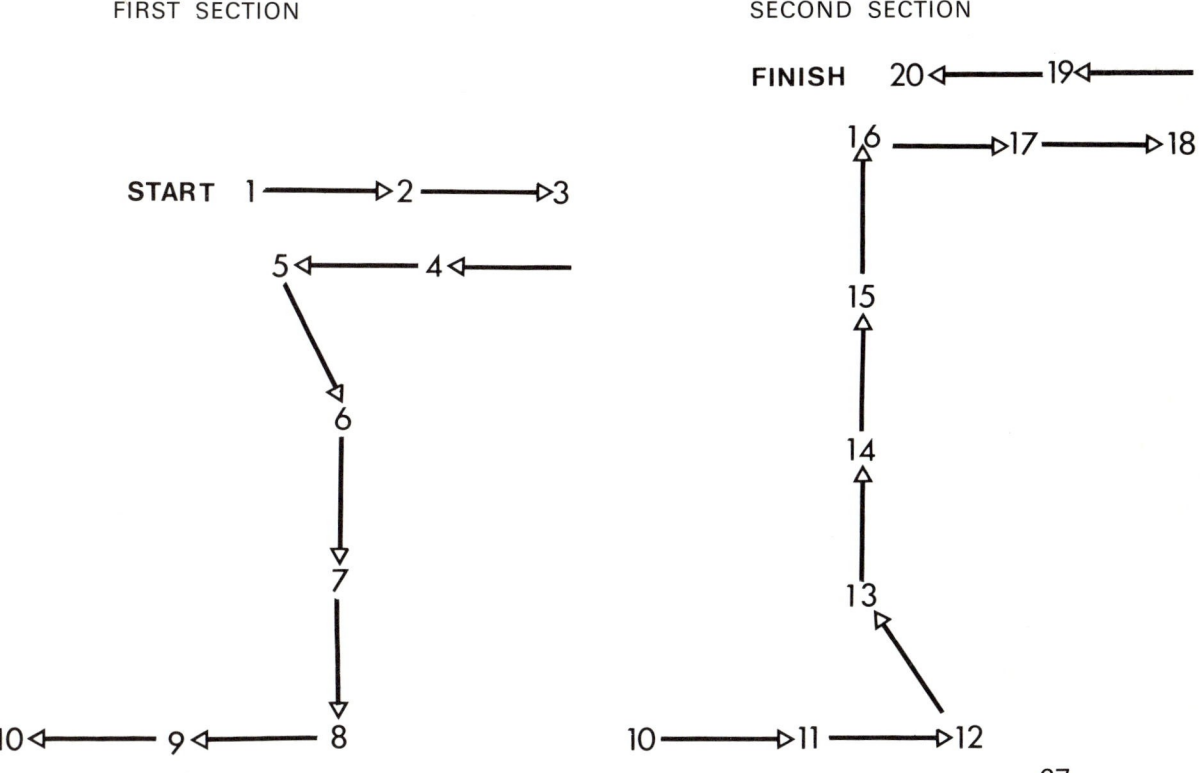

# TAIKYOKU III

Starting position: Fudo-dachi stance.

Move left foot diagonally back; stand on the balls of both feet.

Turn left into back leaning stance, and start left arm middle inside block.

Complete the block.

Bring left foot back into position shown: a forward leaning stance, one shoulder's-width wide and two shoulder's-width deep; begin downward block with left hand, cover with right hand.

Twist hips and legs into forward leaning stance, and complete downward block.

In same stance, step forward and punch upper thrust punch.

Again same stance, step forward and punch upper thrust punch.

Move forward with right leg into forward leaning stance and make middle thrust punch.

Bring front (right) foot back diagonally behind you and start middle inside block with right arm.

Turn into back leaning stance and complete block.

Move forward with left leg into forward leaning stance, and punch middle thrust punch with left hand.

A third step and right hand punch.

Commence 270° turn by moving rear leg to position shown.

Turn into back leaning stance and effect middle inside block.

Complete the block.

| Step forward right leg; punch with right arm. | Using front leg (right leg), move back in opposite direction. Begin middle inside block with right arm. | Complete turn into back leaning stance and block. | Step forward with left leg and punch with left arm. |

| Step forward and punch with right arm again. | Commence 270° turn by sliding back (left) leg into position shown; commence middle inside block with left arm. | Complete turn into back leaning stance, and block. | Step forward with right leg, and punch with right hand. |

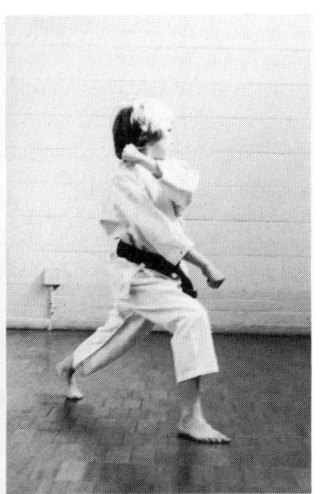   

Move front (left) leg into position shown, ready to turn into forward leaning stance; begin downward block with left arm; cover with right arm.

Complete turn into forward leaning stance, and block.

Step forward and punch with right arm.

Step forward and punch with left arm.

Commence turn into opposite direction by moving front foot diagonally to rear; commence middle inside block.

Complete block and turn.

Move forward with left leg and punch with left arm.

Step back with left foot to original starting position; stand on balls of feet.

Drop heels back on to floor and bring arms down from the position shown, back to ready stance position.

Finish on same spot and in same position as you started.

# 10. Equipment training

Most Karate clubs with good instructors make use of a variety of equipment to help the student progress up the Karate ladder from beginner to black belt. Small clubs often have difficulty in acquiring sandbags or other equipment. This may also be the case if you do not have access to a club for frequent training and have to practise on your own much of the time. We have, therefore, used the second part of this chapter to show how you can substitute everyday objects — even your *Karate gi* itself — for punchbags and sandbags.

The most important and most widely-used piece of equipment found in Karate clubs is the sandbag. The bag is used primarily for *timing* and to gain experience in *distancing* the opponent. Because it will not damage your hand or foot, you need have no apprehension in striking a full blow. Therefore, it allows you to focus the blow *on* the target, which you cannot do in free-fighting or pre-determined fighting sessions in your club. Below are some examples of how you can use sandbags in your training.

Get into a firm position with your weight on the balls of both feet.

Strike with a reverse straight punch. It is useful if your partner can hold the bag to prevent it swinging away.

Back fist strike.

Front kick.

Open hand strike.

Roundhouse kick.

Jumping front kick.

Jumping side kick.

Jumping back kick.

If you do not have access to the type of bags shown in the photographs, other things can be substituted. For example, the *Karate gi* jacket can be very tightly twisted up and used for practising:

Punches.

Front kicks.

Round kicks.

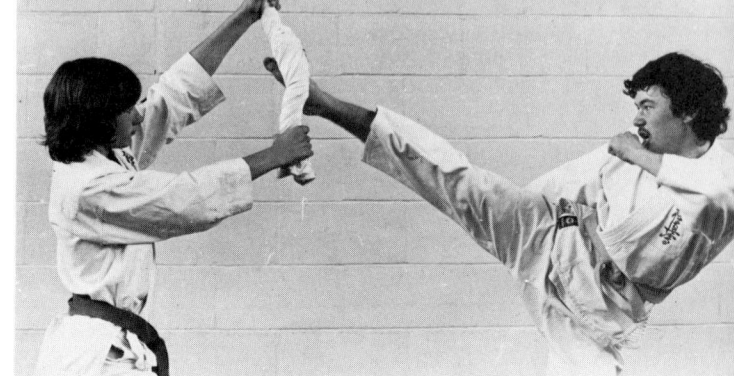

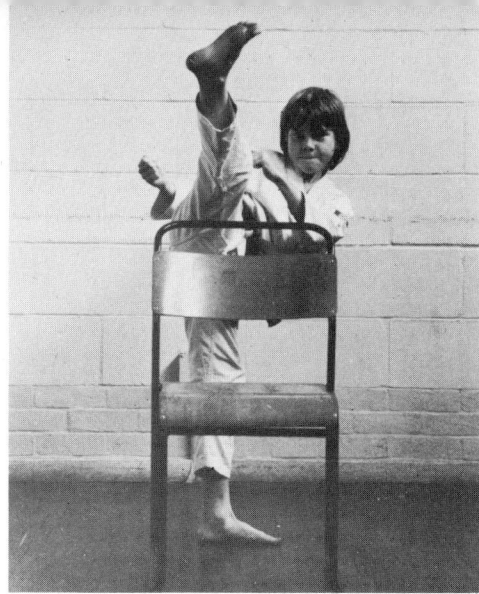

Round kick.

Side kick.

Ordinary kitchen chairs can also be used (see above).

A rubber ball suspended from a string is invaluable to the more experienced student in focusing his kicks on a small target (see below).

Jumping side kick.

Roundhouse kick.

Skipping for fitness.

Jumping to build your legs (above right).

The belt of your *Karate gi* can also be used to assist in general training.

Stretching exercises.

# 11. The Karate training hall and Karate etiquette

## THE KARATE TRAINING HALL (DOJO)

The Karate Training Hall is called the Karate *dojo*. In Japan, until recent years, the senior or grand master of the school lived above the main training hall of the school.

As Karate is practiced with bare feet, the floor of the *dojo* will usually be made of woodblock or some polished wood, and preferably sprung like a gymnasium floor. This prevents cuts or damage to the feet. One wall of the training hall will often be covered with mirrors from ceiling to floor to enable students to check their positions and movements.

If you wish to start Karate training but you are unable to find a hall with a satisfactory polished floor, then the Japanese mats *(tatami),* or the rubber mats used in some judo clubs in Europe, will provide a surface which will be satisfactory enough to enable you to start. At worst, a grassy area in your garden or, if you live near the sea, a sandy beach can give you a temporary training area until you locate an indoor training hall. The drawback of these other surfaces is that, although they will not damage your feet, they will slow up your foot movements. Under normal training conditions your instructor will wish you to make a controlled increase in the speed of your foot movements.

## GRADES AND BELTS

When you join a well-established Karate school, you will see that the big division in members is between the black belts (or *Dan* grades) and all other members, who are not wearing black belts but wear single-coloured belts signifying their *Kyu* grades. Students who have not reached black belt rank are called *Kyu* grades, which means *boy;* black belts are called

*Dan* grades, which means *man,* indicating that the wearer has reached a certain stage of progress and — more important — maturity, in his Karate career. The complete hierarchy of grades in a Karate school is as follows:

| Grade | Belt worn |
| --- | --- |
| Beginner 10th Kyu 9th Kyu | White |
| 8th Kyu 7th Kyu | Blue |
| 6th Kyu 5th Kyu | Yellow |
| 4th Kyu 3rd Kyu | Green |
| 2nd Kyu 1st Kyu | Brown |
| 1st Dan to 5th Dan | Black |
| 6th Dan and above | Red and White |

In the *dojo,* brown belts and 1st and 2nd Dans are called *Sempai,* which means senior grade; 3rd Dans, 4th Dans and 5th Dans are called *Sensei,* which is a very respectful term meaning 'teacher' and is applied to professional people such as lawyers and doctors in Japan. The very rare 6th Dan grade or above is referred to as *Shihan* — 'master'. You are unlikely to be instructed by a Shihan before you yourself reach Dan ranking.

Strict discipline is observed, and great courtesy is shown in the training hall to all members of the school particularly those of Sensei or Shihan rank. It is considered good manners and obligatory for all members to bow on entering and leaving the *dojo,* and at all times upon approaching the senior instructor of the school, whether inside or outside the training hall.

Standing bow on entering the dojo.

Standing bow to the senior instructor.

The class in deep-seated kneeling position.

The bow to the instructor.

Smoking, eating or drinking, swearing and rowdy behaviour are not allowed in the training hall; nor are uncontrolled attacks allowed by students in free-fighting practise if such behaviour and lack of control might result in damage to other students. Any serious breach of the training hall rules and etiquette will result in the offender being expelled and, if on his return to the training hall he persists in the same breach or lack of etiquette and manners, he will be banned from the training hall for some months.

The enforcement of the strict rules of Karate etiquette does not mean that the Karate training hall is a miserable place with the students feeling 'weighed down' by 'oppressive' regulations and out-of-date rules of courtesy—far from it! A well-run *dojo* is a very happy place with an atmosphere found only in martial art schools.

What then, you may ask, is the purpose of these rules of etiquette and why are they so strictly enforced? The answer is that the Karate rules of etiquette are partly tradition and partly for the practical, efficient running of the *dojo*. 'Karate begins and ends with courtesy' is a maxim or saying in all Japanese Karate schools. Karate is, after all, principally a method of combat; many of the techniques taught to higher grade students can kill or seriously injure — the master must, therefore, instruct in an atmosphere of *discipline* and *control,* and ensure that the students, whilst enjoying the training, at the same time appreciate that the techniques must never be used in anger. Students wishing to progress to a high standard must prove that they are responsible people before the master will demonstrate, and instruct in, potentially lethal blows. In some Chinese Boxing *(Kung Fu)* schools, the length of training required to be completed by a student before the *Sifu* (teacher) will feel that the student has demonstrated the correct attitude to the art, enabling him to be taught advanced technique, may be anything up to ten years! The rules of courtesy and discipline are, therefore, for the benefit of the *dojo* members generally, and are intended to make it possible for both individual students and the whole school to concentrate on the training given to them in the right atmosphere.

## SENIOR INSTRUCTOR

The senior *Sensei* in a school is the base on which the school is built.

In *dojos* run on traditional Japanese lines, the *Sensei* is a type of benevolent dictator — a disciplinarian, yet a father to the younger students. The *Sensei* will have the full confidence of his students, and will expect — and will receive — precise and attentive silence from all students. The general atmosphere in the *dojo* depends upon the bearing and personality, as well as the technical ability, of the senior instructor. The ability to instil discipline yet inspire the senior students to realise their real potential is part of the overall requirement for senior black belts, in addition to the necessary ability to teach the techniques of Karate.

## BOWING

Before and after the training session all students will line up in grade order and will kneel and bow to the instructor. The kneeling bow is done at an angle of 30°, with the fists placed on the floor; the eyes look to the front and not downward. The whole bowing movement and return to the deep-seated position is done quickly (see page 81).

In a large *dojo,* where there are many black belts and high grade members, you will find that there will be four separate bows at the end of the training session: to the chief instructor (if he is 6th Dan or above) — on the command *Shihan-ni-Rei;* to the senior instructor (if 3rd Dan or above) — on the command *Sensei-ni-Rei;* to the senior club members on the command *Sempai-ni-Rei.* The instructors will then bow to the class, and the class will return the bow, on the order *Otaga-ni-Rei.*

While the whole Karate system of etiquette — and particularly the bowing procedure described above — may at first be considered archaic by young Europeans and Americans who are unused to the discipline of the martial arts, the atmosphere in a properly run *dojo* soon transfers itself to the very newest entrants, who begin to understand the reason for the discipline and the true function of the instructor, which is not only to teach technique but also to create harmony in the *dojo* and to motivate students to achieve the best possible standard.

## THE KARATE GI OR TRAINING OUTFIT

The *gi* consists of a jacket (with short sleeves), trousers and belt. The

Karate outfit is made of lighter material than the judo *gi,* as it suffers less physical pulling and general wear.

## Tying the belt

Place belt at waist, leaving good lengths on each side.

Wind belt around your waist and bring both ends to the front.

Bring right end under left and other layer, and pull firm.

Take left end over right and pull tight. The knot is a reef knot.

# Folding the gi after use

The Karate gi laid out.

First fold in the sleeves, then fold the jacket to the centre.

Roll very tightly.

Tie with the belt as shown above.

Your outfit should be kept clean and repaired at all times. A student who allows his outfit to become dirty and whose general appearance is untidy will soon become unpopular in the training hall, and people will not wish to train with him. This creates discord and lack of harmony in the *dojo.* For the same reason fingernails, toenails and hair should be kept short and clean—long nails can cause unwelcome accidents in the *dojo.* Long hair is not forbidden, but students with longer than shoulder-length hair are normally instructed to have this held back from the face by a hairband.

If you do not possess a Karate suit, a loose-fitting jacket and a pair of old trousers or an athletics track-suit will provide a satisfactory substitute for the time being.

# 12. Choosing a Karate school

If you wish to make a success of your Karate training, there are certain things that you should do:
- (a) Find a well-run Karate school with a real martial arts atmosphere.
- (b) Be prepared to organise your free time so that you are able to devote a certain amount of time to attending the *dojo* for training, and allot other time for training out of school.
- (c) Reach a fair degree of all-round physical fitness and maintain this.
- (d) Adopt the mental attitude which will best aid your progress in the art.

**FINDING A GOOD TEACHER AND SCHOOL**

The importance of a good teacher and Karate school in your progress cannot be overemphasised. Unfortunately finding these is easier said than done, and we realize the problem which will face you in selecting a school if you have no knowledge of the various styles and schools available to you. Regrettably, due to the recent 'explosion' in the popularity of Karate, which has happened at a time when there are few qualified instructors available to teach the growing number of people wanting instruction, many unqualified people have set up schools to take advantage of the situation. In some cases these individuals have even awarded themselves black belts of high degree! Such grades are, of course, worthless and any grades which such individuals award to students have no standing in the Karate world.

How does a potentially serious student avoid the Karate phoney or con-man? The best advice which we can give is that you should check that the instructor of the club which you are thinking of joining holds a British Karate Control Commission (B.K.C.C.) Certificate and, therefore, belongs to one of the major Karate styles represented on the Commission. The Commission is the Government-backed body which, as its name suggests, controls the administration and growth of Japanese-style Karate in the United Kingdom. The addresses and telephone numbers of the Commission and the main Karate Associations in Great Britain, Australia, Canada and the United States are given at the end of this book. The largest and best-known of the Japanese Karate styles in the United Kingdom are *Kyokushinkai* (Oyama school), *Shotokan* (Japan Karate Association), *Goju-kai* and *Wado-ryu.* There is not a great deal of difference between the major Japanese styles — although, whichever of the styles you finally join, you will notice that it will claim to be unchallengeably the best! In any event, Great Britain has for some years fielded a National Karate Team drawn from all the B.K.C.C. styles, so that the top instructors and grades of each style are usually acquainted with the basic strengths, weaknesses and particular techniques of the different styles.

If you find a *dojo* in which there is an obvious lack of discipline, where — even to your inexperienced eye — the students and teachers appear to treat each other with less than the degree of respect which you would expect, or where the Karate kits are grubby and the general bearing of the members and the whole *dojo* atmosphere seem not to be such as to create the right environment for learning — then look for another *dojo*. There are well-run Karate schools in nearly every town of any size in England, and this situation will soon be true of Wales and Scotland as well; you may, however, have to search a little before finding the best school in your area.

## TRAINING

Having found the best school which is available to you, how often should you train and what supplemental training, other than pure Karate training, should you do to make the fastest progress?

It is fairly easy to be definite about the first question; less easy with the second. You should train as often as you can, as long as it does not adversely affect your main obligations such as school, college, your job or your family and home life. Even if you are able to attend your Karate school only once a week, one of the advantages of Karate as a sport is that you can practise many of the techniques – and particularly the Kata – on your own. Full-time students at Karate schools in Japan or Korea will normally train for two separate two- or three-hour sessions each day. Naturally, where such an intense degree of training is being carried on, the sessions will be very varied in order to retain the students' interest and concentration. In actual hours, it is better to train five times a week for one hour per session, than twice a week with a $2\frac{1}{2}$-hour session each time.

Do not train immediately after a heavy meal. You will certainly suffer discomfort and you may even be sick.

On the days that you do not train, try to do something totally different from Karate. However dedicated you may become to your training routine, Karate must not be the only thing in your life. The ancient masters of the martial arts were also painters, poets, inventors and philosophers. A truly balanced person needs a variety of interests to find success in living.

With regard to the second question, any form of physical exercise which promotes better physical conditioning and increased bodily strength must be good for your general improvement in Karate, in the same way as it would in most sports. So rugby, football, swimming, athletics, basketball and other popular sports will help your Karate progress, provided your Karate training still takes precedence. Some sports or activities are particularly useful to Karate students. Gymnastics and ballet both build the strong yet supple muscles which are the aim of Karate training also, but which take upwards of several months of hard work to achieve. Sprinting, which is an 'explosive' event, is also good training, as it will help your reactions to speed up, and it will also help to build strong leg muscles, which are very important for good balance and strong stances in Karate.

What about training with weights? Basically, weight training under proper supervision in order to gain *strength* must be good for you. Care should be taken, however, to see that you do not fall into the trap of spending too much of your spare time on weight training to the detriment of your Karate training routine. Your weight training must always remain subsidiary to your Karate training.

A good standard of physical fitness will certainly be achieved within a short time of your commencing Karate training. Most people who begin Karate are unfit — even though they may play football or netball on Saturday afternoons! Within two months, however, you will reach a good standard of fitness and a much improved feeling of well-being.

At first the exercises shown to the beginners are intended to loosen the muscles and tendons rather than to make you stronger. Once you have achieved the necessary degree of suppleness needed for Karate techniques, the exercises will be extended to include strengthening exercises to prepare you for the more rigorous training which your programme will include as you approach the higher grades and particularly the *Sempai* (brown and 1st Dan black belt) grades. Generally, all-round fitness is required and the only area on which your instructor will place particular emphasis is the legs and hips. The Japanese have over the centuries created highly-developed legs and hips, due mainly to the position in which they sit or squat on their heels — even today. It is difficult for western people to achieve comparable leg-development without specific exercises being utilised to stretch the tendons of the legs and hips; such exercises will be taught to you during your early training days at the *dojo*. Many of these exercises will be similar to the leg- and hip-stretching movements in Yoga. Chapter 3 shows you the exercises which you will need to practise to obtain the suppleness required for maximum progress.

Once you have reached the degree of fitness your instructor wants, and you will feel this yourself without having to be told, you must try to maintain this. If possible, work through some of the exercises every day. Ten or fifteen minutes put aside each day will keep your body supple and fit for training at any time, and will prevent stiffness between training sessions.

## MENTAL ATTITUDE

The most important factor in your success in Karate is *your attitude:* your attitude towards the *dojo,* towards the etiquette and towards the *Sensei.* To succeed in anything worth mastering you need *dedication* and *perseverance,* whether it be learning the piano, studying for university entrance or a degree — or the study of a martial art. Your instructor will take little interest in you at first. This is normal in the martial arts. He wants you to prove that you are a serious student, a person to whom he will be pleased to impart his knowledge. As you progress so he will spend more time helping you to understand the techniques and why they are done. Once you have obtained his respect, he will seek to motivate and direct you to discover yourself — not necessarily in his own mould, but rather to help you develop in your own way.

But, however good your instructor is and however fast your initial progress, at some stage you will become bored by the amount of repetition of basic technique which your instructor will require you to do. This is particularly so in the middle grades, about half-way between beginner and black belt. However interesting your instructor makes the training sessions, there is a certain amount of good hard 'slogging' work needed, which undeniably all students sooner or later find boring — indeed the greatest loss of students from Karate schools takes place when this period in the training arrives. The best way to deal with this is to concentrate extra hard on each technique; try to perfect or improve some particular *aspect* of each stance, strike or kick even though at the time your mental boredom may have temporarily convinced you that no progress is being made. Within a few sessions you will cast off the period of boredom and once again look forward to training, and also begin to notice genuine improvements in your Karate.

As a serious student you will realise that, apart from your *dojo* training, it will be an advantage for you to do some Karate training outside school to ensure maximum progress. As with all sports, the movements that should be practised in extra training time are those which you find most difficult to master, so that at the next *dojo* session you will have made some improvement, thus enabling the instructor to move on to new techniques. It is particularly useful for you to make your own sandbag and hang this up in the garden at home, because in the *dojo* there is often insufficient time for all the students to practise kicks for as long as the instructor would like.

To get you and the other students out of the *dojo,* most of the larger Karate schools hold both winter and summer *Gashikus,* which are one- or two-day training sessions held either in the country or on the coast. These special training sessions are at the same time hard work and great fun, with the instructors and black belts training beside the beginners. Understandably the summer session is normally better attended than the winter session!

Finally, and most important, you must accept that your progress in Karate will depend upon the intensity with which you devote yourself to constant practise. Achieving self-fulfillment through Karate can be done only by developing this great concentration, whether it is called will-power or focus and known in Karate terminology as *Kiai.* The development of intense concentration whereby the body can achieve the apparently impossible is known as developing 'one's own iron will'.

Summer Gashiku training in the country.

# Glossary of Japanese Karate terminology

| | | | |
|---|---|---|---|
| *Age* or *Ago* | Rising | *Kakato-geri* | Heel kick |
| *Ago-uchi* | Rising strike or upper-cut | *Kanzetsu-geri* | Kick to knee |
| | | *Karateka* | Person who studies Karate |
| *Ashi* | Leg | | |
| *Ashiwaza* | Leg and foot technique | *Karate gi* | The Karate suit |
| | | *Kata* | Pre-arranged forms of demonstrating methods of attack, defence and counter-attack. |
| *Chudan* | Middle | | |
| *Chudan-tsuki* | Middle thrust punch | | |
| *Chudan-uchi-uke* | Middle inside block | | |
| *Chudan-soto-uke* | Middle outside block | *Ke-age* | High forward kick |
| *Chusoku* | Ball of foot | *Keri-waza* | Kicking technique |
| | | *Kiba-dachi* | Horse stance |
| *Empi* | Elbow | *Kokutsu-dachi* | Back leaning stance |
| | | *Kote* | Forearm |
| *Fudo-dachi* | Normal stance | *Kumite* | Contest |
| *Fumikomi* | Stamping technique with foot | *Koken-uchi* | Chicken-head strike |
| | | *Mae-geri* | Front kick with ball of foot |
| *Gedan-barai* | Downward parry | | |
| *Gyaku* | Reverse | *Makiwara* | Karate punching board |
| *Haisoku-dachi* | Stance with feet together | *Mawashi* | Circular or turning |
| | | *Mawashi-geri* | Roundhouse kick |
| *Heiko-dachi* | Parallel stance | *Mawashi-uke* | Roundhouse block |
| *Heisoku* | Instep of foot | *Mawatte* | The order to reverse the direction of a movement |
| *Hiji-ate* | Elbow attack | | |
| *Hiraken* | Flat or level fist | | |
| *Hiza* | Knee | *Morote-uke* | Block using one arm to support the other |
| *Hiza-ganmen-geri* | Knee strike to face | | |
| | | *Musubi-dachi* | Stance with heels together but feet open |
| *Jodan* | Upper | | |
| *Jiyu Kumite* | Free sparring | | |
| *Juji-uke* | Cross block | *Nukite* | Finger strike |
| *Jun-tsuki* | Side thrust punch | *Neko-ashi dachi* | Cat stance |

| | | | |
|---|---|---|---|
| *Nogare* | Special breathing technique | | body-control exercises) |
| | | *Tettsui* | Hammerfist |
| *Oi tsuki* | Pursuit thrust punch | | |
| *Oroshi* | Downward blow | *Uchihachiji-dachi* | Pigeon-toe shoulder-wide stance |
| *Sanchin-dachi* | Hour-glass stance | *Uchi-uke* | Inside block |
| *Seiken* | Normal fist | *Uke* | Block or parry |
| *Shotei* | Palm of hand | *Uraken* | Inverted or back fist |
| *Shuto* | Edge of hand, swordhand | *Uraken yoko ganmen uchi* | Back fist side strike |
| *Shihan* | Master of Karate | *Uraken shomen uchi* | Back fist strike forward to face |
| *Shiko-dachi* | Sumo stance | | |
| *Soto-uke* | Outer block | | |
| *Sukui-uke* | Scooping block | *Uraken hizo uchi* | Back fist strike to spleen |
| *Sokuto* | Knife foot used in side kicks | *Ushiro-geri* | Back kick |
| *Tate-tsuki* | Vertical hand punch | *Yoko-geri* | Side thrust kick |
| *Te* | Hand | *Yoko-keage* | High side kick |
| *Tobi-geri* | Jumping kick | | |
| *Tsuki* | Thrust | *Zenkutsu-dachi* | Forward leaning stance |
| *Taikyoku* | Simple Kata (lit. | | |

# Karate Organizations and Associations

## GREAT BRITAIN

### Controlling Bodies

The General Secretary,
The British Karate Control Commission,
4/16 Deptford Bridge,
London SE8 4JS.

The Secretary,
Scottish Karate Board of Control,
4 Queensferry Street,
Edinburgh EH2 4PB.

The Secretary,
Welsh Karate Board of Control,
44 Albert Street,
Miskin, Mountain Ash,
Glamorgan.

### Main Associations (this list is not exhaustive)

British Karate Kyokushinkai
(Oyama Ryu)
Gen. Sec: 37 Winchester Avenue,
Walderslade, Chatham,
Kent.

*or:* The Chairman,
B.K.K.,
8 Warren Road,
Purley, Surrey.

British Gojuryu Karate Association,
Sec: 48 Sutherland Road,
Worsley Mesnes, Wigan,
Lancs.

United Kingdom Karate Wado-Kai,
Gen. Sec: 11 Wren Street,
Burnley, Lancs.

Shukokai K. Association,
c/o R. Stanhope,
59 Millbrook Avenue,
Shirley Park,
Denton, Manchester.

Karate Union of Great Britain (Shotokan),
Sec: C. Hepburn,
5 Darley Road,
Manchester N16 0DG.

## AUSTRALIA

### Controlling Body

Australian Karate Control Commission,
c/o R. Bolton,
15/24 East Esplanade,
Manly 295, N.S.W.

## CANADA

### Controlling Body

Canadian Karate,
c/o T. Suruoka,
Bucks 788,
Station S, Toronto.

# UNITED STATES OF AMERICA
## Controlling Body

The Secretary,
National A.A.U. Karate Committee,
Amateur Athletic Union, U.S.A.,
A.A.U. House,
3400 West 86 Street,
Indianapolis, Indiana 46268.

The number of different Karate Associations and clubs in N. America is legion. The undermentioned are some of the more prominent:

Kyokushinkai (U.S.A.),
c/o T. Nakamura,
135 West 14 Street,
New York, N.Y. 10011.

Japan Karate Federation (U.S.A.),
1429 N. Bristol,
Santa Anna, California.

Goju Ryu Karate Association,
24 North Augusta Street,
Staunton, Virginia.

Shotokai Kawanabe Karate Association,
8801 North Riviera Drive,
Tucson, Arizona.

Int'L Karate-do Association,
2582 East Colorado Street,
Pasadena, California.

Yoseikan Chito-kai Karate Federation,
22 Martin Street,
Covington, Kentucky.

Uechi Ryu Karate Association,
153 Weybosset Street,
Providence, Rhode Island.

Shorin Ryu Karate Association,
832 San Mateo,
S.E. Albuquerque,
New Mexico.

Isshin Ryu Karate Association,
5243 South Tacoma Way,
Tacoma, Washington State.

Wadokai Karate Association,
c/o Ryokichi Katano,
Lockview Plaza,
Main Street,
Lockport, N.Y.

All American Hapkido Federation,
1128 South Western Avenue,
Los Angeles, California.

Gojukai Karate-do Association,
97 Collingswood Street,
San Francisco, California.

Shotokan Karate of America (West),
4300 Melrose Avenue,
Los Angeles, California.

Kenpo Karate Association,
Ed Parker,
1705 East Walnut Street,
Pasadena, Ca 91106,
California.

Shotokan Karate of America (East),
1315 Newport Gap Pike,
Wilmington, Delaware.

United States Karate Association,
1134 South Woodward Avenue,
Royal Oak, Michigan.

All Japan Karate-do Association (U.S.A.),
1245 Main Avenue Clifton,
New Jersey.